Published by Semiotext(e)
PO BOX 629. South Pasadena, CA 91031
www.semiotexte.com

Cover Art by Christine Pichini
Frontpiece: Hans Georg Berger, *L'atélier de Balthus.*
Archive Nr G055-12A
www.hansgeorgberger.de

Design by Hedi El Kholti
ISBN: 978-1-58435-199-3

Distributed by The MIT Press, Cambridge, Mass. and, London, England

CRAZY FOR VINCENT

Hervé Guibert

Translated by Christine Pichini
Introduction by Bruce Hainley

semiotext(e)

Bruce Hainley

Notes on *Fou de Vincent*

(for *Nicolas Pages*)

Right now I am looking at a photograph of Hervé
Guibert and Vincent. As rendered by Guibert's friend,
photographer and writer Hans Georg Berger, both men
are young, although Vincent, as he would be until his
friend died too young, was younger. Guibert was only
ever young, even as he became relentlessly *clock-haunted*.
In the picture, Vincent exudes swagger, and tough-guy
attitude. When I texted the picture to C.P., she texted
back that Guibert "is sitting because V. is so short," lover
gently drawing attention away from his loved one's
compactness to direct focus on his foxy bod. Was
Vincent always, as he looks here—standing in pleated
slacks, legs rakishly crossed, shirtless—ready for anything? Think James Cagney in *The Public Enemy* or *Lady*

(7)

Killer. His left arm akimbo, Vincent faces Berger's camera as he leans his right on a work table, the look on his face proudly acknowledging how the classical statuary behind him—rugged torso, virile bust—only reflects his dominion. Off to his right, Guibert, seated on a low chair perhaps made for a child, almost swallowed by shadow but more than content, holds his left pointer finger to his lips, keeping mum on all he might say about the transferences and countertransferences prowling the scene, which is *"dans l'atélier de Balthus."*—a studio privy to the cerebral, feline waywardness that would produce a painterly *jeune fille* now coursing with the unruly brio of the *jeune étalon.* I won't point out just how many grim things hadn't happened yet in the world when they posed for the picture.

*

Tequila, Congolese grass, cocaine, heroin, licorice-colored opium, hashish, bison grass vodka, beer, mezcal, champagne, poppers, ecstasy, expensive perfume or Vincent's home-brewed vanilla-nutmeg concoction: "My relationship with Vincent," Guibert wagers at a low point, "can only exist through drugs." But he's just as much addicted to love, or crashing from that high— and his *récit*'s "on" Vincent. Some kind of hair of the dog, "[w]riting about him is an appeasement."

*

I'm crazy for trying and crazy for crying and I'm crazy for loving you, Patsy Cline lamented, sang, aflame. Let everything her voice conveys in that song deliver the most exacting gloss on *Crazy for Vincent* and its portrait of unlikely desire, of desiring and the grisaille of difference that constitutes it. "I watch porn videos with girls in them sitting next to him…I watch alongside him one of the images that moves me the most, a boy who licks a cock that moves in and out of a vagina…"

*

From *The Mausoleum of Lovers*:

> "The other day, I was thinking again of the wish voiced by M.P. that I make a sequel to *Voyage avec deux enfants*, a book I would call *Vincent*, that I would extract from this journal. I took the last two notebooks to assemble from them, through reading, the disjointed, scattered traces; and that day I told myself that this reconstitution would risk being somewhat filthy. It's Vincent's effects on my life that are touching, more than a continuity?"

*

Vincent's self-described "ugly face" and "beautiful torso," *angelus novus* versus monster, i.e., Buster Keaton vs. Boris Karloff; Vincent's saliva, "precious commodity that he spits on the street"—lubricant, profligacy, punctuating device; Vincent's funguses, scabies, herpes, and lice, the "pathetic little shit," his "geisho," is sometimes practically leprous: "[h]oles in his skin, on his fingers, on his chin. Depigmentation of certain zones on his back." And yet, as Vincent's "Guibertino" writes, "I pulled his body against mine"—against, as C.P. reminded me, H.G.'s "ugly" torso and beautiful face.

*

Crazy for Vincent contains the articulation, is, in some way, about the impossibility of not articulating, finally, even if only in passing, that acrid acronym, AIDS, that new condition—one of Guibert's two books, both published in July 1989, to mention the infection, point-blank, for the first time. *L'Incognito*, a murder mystery set amid hustler bars and gay clubs, is the other. Dead bodies propel both.

*

Run-on sentences accumulate because the author doesn't wish thinking about Vincent to stop, textual Vincentness to cease.

*

(10)

Soon after finishing work on his only film, *La Pudeur ou l'Impudeur* [*Modesty, or Immodesty*], Guibert was interviewed for *Le nouvel observateur* by Didier Eribon. At the end of the interview, published in July 1991, Eribon asks:

> D.E.: What do you think of Michel Foucault's sentence about you in the preface he wrote for the Duane Michals' catalogue? He speaks of "those forms of work which don't advance like an oeuvre, but which open up because they are experiences." He mentions Magritte, *Under the Volcano, Der Tod der Maria Malibran,* Bob Wilson, and he ends: "And of course H.G."

> H.G.: I find that very fair with regard to what I've tried to do. At the point where I get in a state to write a book, literature incurs my wrath. [...]

> D.E.: This "experience" isn't therefore solely a literary one. There's intervention from the world outside?

> H.G.: There's the experience of writing, and that's the point where I become Hervé Guibert, the character in my books. I often have the impression of leading a double life. When people

stop me in the street—"Aren't you Hervé Guibert?"—I feel like responding: "No, I'm not Hervé Guibert right now." Because at just that moment, I'm not caught in a wave of immodesty, in that strange intercourse there is between experience and writing.

Experiences open up; some works, rather than plotting advances straightforwardly, double that experiential opening up and in doing so trouble it. In passing, Foucault had pinpointed something vital in his friend's (H.G.'s) procedures, those that the dull would too quickly simplify, or quarantine in the ward of "autofiction"; instead the philosopher encourages the questions burrowed within the intercourse between experience and writing to rendezvous with their question marks. H.G. doesn't stop at self-reflection, but somehow passes through it, Alice-like. Which Guibert is the one any reader hails in H.G.'s texts, since the process of their reading might involve almost as much immodesty as their writing. "[H]ere again the character of a novel insinuates itself in me."

*

This immodest wave, *this strange intercourse between experience and writing*: it's what Vincent comes to represent for the author and what Vincent wishes to evade. "I have the impression of leading a double life": H.G. both wants Vincent and to write him, which, while not exactly the same thing as fucking him or being fucked by him might be *fucking him over*, his model both relishes the attention and resents it. "He must be afraid to face me: stage fright of becoming my character again." That wave of immodesty—*"une vague d'impudeur"* is how H.G. puts it—the wave's, in part, Vincent's, or a secret sign for Vincent. Rising up in the interview with Eribon, the wave points to those green times of Breton-like *amour fou*, when the lover wishes to insinuate the loved one into every instant, every bit of the world seeming to instigate murmuring invocation of the loved one; that time is not often forever. Too unbearable to have Vincent's participation in his life be merely fiction: thus the ritual killing that starts the book, offing one Vincent so that another Vincent (fictional? tractable?) can enter the scene, allowing the inter-course to continue. Late in the *récit*, Guibert writes: "For an hour, Vincent tells me about a wave—the way to take it, to ride it or be crushed by it, how to be at one with it; I tremble with fear, feeling death coil between us." Vincent might be a kind of muse, but that doesn't mean he wishes to become an inverted Galatea-thing, immobilized in the coma of represen-tation. The author and his model are equally freaked out by the prospect. "From now on, in my datebook, out of superstition, I add a question mark after his first name."

*

Late last summer, I bought a first edition of *Fou de Vincent.* The bookseller described the state of his copy of the book in this way: *"Edition originale sans grand papier. Exemplaire proprement coupé (cette première edition était parue non coupée, en raison du caractère sulfureux de certaines pages)."* I wondered exactly what pages some authority might have found of a sulfurous nature. Unseemly enough for the pages of the book's first issue to remain *non coupée.*

*

About Vincent's cock, H.G. relays many aspects: it's beloved and bite-sized. It has properties both "aqueous" and of "dust." When Vincent dances "to Prince's 'Kiss' with his cock in [Guibert's] mouth," it's a pro-vision of joyful abandon. While he never reveals whether one root of his obsession is cut or uncut, H.G. does relate its flavor: "Last night, Vincent's cock tasted like fresh paper in the books from the *Bibliotheque Verte."* C.P. notes in her caring translation that the *Bibliotheque Verte* was a "popular French series of chil-dren's books." Was the piquancy of the metaphor and

(14)

all it suggests deemed unsuitable for public consump-
tion, *sulfureux*? How old is Vincent anyway? He's
described at one point as "a child too old to be my son,
too young to be my brother." When Vincent "reread
my book, *Voyage avec deux enfants*, he said that it showed
him how disgraceful his character is." But his is not
the only character in the book and certainly not the
only one considering his disgracefulness or immodesty.
"When I wake up, hemmed in by the traces of that
body I worshipped, that disappeared, I'm ready to
rinse out my mouth with ammonia and powder the
sheets and his pillow with sulphur."

*

Literature incurs H.G.'s wrath. By way of his truth-
telling? By his admitting his desire as quasi-pedophilic?
By his desublimating and/or deidealizing explicitnesses?
By his resisting laws of genre, dissolving the prophy-
lactic barriers between fact/fiction? In the interview
with Eribon, H.G. invokes the works of Pierre Guyotat.
He singles out "*Cobra* by Severo Sarduy, a hysterical,
baroque book, a book of a crazy queen, that I adored,
that truly impressed me." Unmentioned: Tony Duvert's
Journal d'un innocent, which must in some way have held
a powerful sway. H.G. recalls his passion for Roland
Barthes, and although he states that "*Fou de Vincent* is
deeply inspired by *Fragments d'un discours amoureux*,"

it's somehow his more complicated relation to *Roland Barthes*, both text and person (text as person? Vice versa?), which might be more telling, despite the fact that he claims that it's "perhaps not his best book." *Roland Barthes* opens with a sentence delivered in a facsimile of Barthes' handwriting: *"Tout ceci doit être considéré comme dit par un personnage de roman."* ("It must all be considered as if spoken by a character in a novel.")

*

More than anything else, it might be Guibert's textual embodiments which kept sulfurous pages sealed, the unnerving, immodest intercourse he trafficked in, more and more intently once his focus hove to his own body, living with AIDS. In *Crazy for Vincent*, Vincent's cock becomes the emblem of the strange intercourse between experience and writing: "always Vincent's cock, like a madness, like a fiction."

*

Elsewhere in H.G.'s work, the emblem's Pinocchio. The funny little Italian poppet adjudicates on much of the later part of *Modesty, or Immodesty*: Pinocchio, in the form of a wooden statuette of the famous puppet the writer Eugène Savitzkaya gave to Guibert. Umberto

Eco praised Carlo Collodi's *Pinocchio* as an "untrustworthy book." The puppet-boy is, of course, disobedient, and he cries a lot when he's gotten into trouble, almost always some consequence of troubling the truth. In what is arguably the most infamous scene of *Modest, or Immodesty*, Guibert plays Russian roulette with two water glasses, one drugged with a mortal dose of digitaline—as Pinocchio stares him down. Despite H.G.'s own gift for writing untrustworthy texts, his prismatic disobedience, no commentary on his work considers Pinocchio as his possible doppelgänger (or an apparition of a certain type he desires), despite the little trickster's appearance in his novels, journals, photographs, and in the video. Formed from magic wood—and I'll leave the erotics of that implicit, only recalling what untrustworthy magic erections are—transubstantiated from wooden marionette into actual boy, a character who has trouble with the truth, consider all that Pinocchio could come to stand for across H.G.'s project. Paul de Man reminded anyone who'd looked the other way that the "aesthetic power is located neither in the puppet nor in the puppeteer but in the text that spins itself between them." As H.G. records in *Les Gangsters*: "One day Vincent told me: 'I am happy to get you to write, that you write thanks to me.'" Of course, no longer a plaything, the puppet's alive, but now, *voilà*, subject to the precariousness of all flesh.

*

"I come across several photos of Vincent that I never printed. I struggle with the mystery of the violence of this love—the photographs remind me strongly of this—and I tell myself that I would like to describe it with the solemnity due the sacred, as if it were one of the great religious mysteries. The tongues of flame, for example, that fall on the apostles."

*

What's it all about, someone might ask. At one point, Vincent's mother instead of her son answers the phone, and the author records the urge his protagonist, Hervé Guibert, has to confess the reason for his call: "It's about his cock, Madame, I need to suck it as soon as possible."

*

From *The Mausoleum of Lovers* (written long after *Fou de Vincent* appeared):

> Vincent has just called, the happiness I felt at
> hearing him was almost unbearable. Restored
> my confidence in both life and death, when just
> now both life and death seemed impossible for

me. Then I told myself that the force of my
love for Vincent had less force than the force of
my illness.

When he arrived, he got out a flick-knife to cut
one by one the pages of my book.

CRAZY FOR VINCENT

In the middle of the night between the 25th and 26th of November, Vincent fell from the third floor playing parachute with a bathrobe. He drank a liter of tequila, smoked Congolese grass, snorted cocaine. Finding him unconscious, his friends call the fire squad. Vincent suddenly recovered, walked to his car, took off. The firemen chase after him, rush into his building, go up with him in the elevator, enter his bedroom; Vincent insults them. He yells, "Let me sleep," them: "You moron, you may never wake up." In the bedroom across the hall, his parents continue to sleep. Vincent threw the firemen out. He fell asleep like a charm. At eight forty-five, his mother shakes him to wake him up for work, he doesn't move an inch, she drives him to the hospital. On the 27th of November, once notified by Pierre, I visited Vincent at Our Lady of Perpetual Help. Two days later, he died of complications from a ruptured spleen.

I had met Vincent in 1982, when he was still a child. He remained in my dreams; I had to resolve that once he became a man, I would continue to love him for what he no longer was. For six years, he invaded my journal. Several months after his death, I decided to find him again in these notes, in reverse.

What was it? A passion? A love? An erotic obsession? Or one of my inventions?

Saw, in the window of a magic shop, a flying saucer made of black bakelite that creates a hologram through an arrangement of lenses and mirrors. You place an object in its cavity, a gold coin or a ring, and its ghost is projected on top of the transparent lid. It seems as if you could steal it; it's unfathomable. I'm tempted to buy the machine to capture something within it that

belongs to Vincent and that, by way of this strange illusion, will remind me of him, but nothing I can think of
(a lock of hair, a photograph) will appease me. Only his
sex would belong in the reliquary.

I never comb my hair; I rub my wet head in a towel then
rake through the curls with my fingers to style it.
Yesterday, I don't know why, I noticed the little comb
that Vincent gave me sitting alone on the bathroom
shelf (he gave me so few things). I picked it up, I
combed my hair, the comb became enchanted. Vincent
had buried the key to the spell in the comb: "If you need
me one day, comb your hair, and I will come." I listen
carefully, but the telephone doesn't ring. The next day,
I comb my hair again: the comb only regains its magic
after the second rake. The day after that I comb my hair
again: it only becomes magical after the third, et cetera.

At Sélect, in the back room, where I change places
several times before he arrives so as to be relaxed as
possible, I make him a declaration. He lowers his eyes,
smiles solemnly, without awkwardness, without sar-
casm; my pain seems to soothe him in the times when
I am most desperate.

I would like to have that sort of heroism that, without bitching and moaning, without giving it a name, consists of suppressing the more or less tolerable absence of his body and embracing another in return, like a retaliatory spell, an intolerable lack that he would suffer from that embrace, and that would make him run to me.

He left, I couldn't wait, I had had enough. I let Hans Georg go with him on the bus to pick up Hector at the airport; I had coordinated his arrival with Vincent's departure. When I come back to my studio, I find a note from him sitting on the bureau, incredibly affectionate, with a drawing; he calls me Guibertino, thanks me for having put up with him. He got some sun, slept, ate well, got his health back, says he's going to stop with the coke. We take Hector to a Rameau concert at *Saint-Louis-les-Francais*, I get bored, think about Vincent sitting on the airplane, we decide to leave at the intermission. Vincent pops up from behind a column. At first I thought I had seen a ghost. Then, he had decided to stay to live with me in Rome. Then, he couldn't get on the airplane. I had made sure the night before to confirm his return flight with the travel agent. He's carrying his luggage on his back; we walk out in front of the church. The airplane was overbooked, and the pilot hadn't wanted to take him in the cabin once he had gotten a look at him. Vincent is with the head of the charter, who escorted him to the church and has offered to pay for him to spend the night in a swanky hotel to make up for it, they'll put him on the first flight to Paris the following morning, Vincent has to start work again that same day, he doesn't know yet that he's been fired. Hector pulls me aside and asks, "Who's that?" I say, "That's Vincent." He exclaims, "That's Vincent?" His tone says, "Yeah, right, that's Vincent!"

The first sentence I wrote about Vincent, at the end of the night I first met him: "Of all the children, I'll go towards the one whose charm is least evident and I will kiss the freckles on his face, all the beauty marks on his hips and the nape of his neck."

Last night he tried to fuck me for an hour, on my stomach, on my side, with cream, on my back underneath him, with a different cream, with the oil he sent me to fetch from the kitchen, but not standing up, since he's too short. I wanted a condom, it was pink with a reservoir, when I took it out of its wrapper to put it on him I asked, "Does that have a meaning?" He said, "You seem to know all about it, that's scary." He wanted to take off the condom, he said, "You're really terrified of catching AIDS, huh?" I couldn't stop apologizing, claiming that my ass was too tight, too dry. He lost his hard-on. At one point he was lying on top of me, he had grabbed my legs to hook them over his shoulders, he whispered, "Arch your back." I couldn't possibly get a cramp; I had become a contortionist. He moaned, he was inside, he sought out my mouth, his tongue pushed inside, I felt like a woman he was fucking. He kissed me a second time, his mouth was dry, he drenched me with saliva, his precious commodity, what he spits on the street.

A strange feeling, to continue writing a book that I gave to my editor six months ago, whose contract has already been signed: writing on loose pages without typing them out and gradually bringing or sending them to the editor as they come, a way of reducing the distance between oneself and the book, to be even closer to it, even deeper inside of it, as if writing directly on the book.

When he found out that, in the end, I had finally opened the letter that Pierre had sent to him at my address, no reproach, only, "Now I know you're really strange."

I had gone to bed early, the others were in the living room, they hadn't heard the telephone, I was sleeping, I got up to answer it, it was Vincent, I didn't recognize his voice because he sounded so good, he asked, "Is it the same time there?" He explained that he hadn't come with us because he found a job as a grip on a film shoot, he said that there were stars in it, got their names wrong, added that he had gained ten kilos, he talked to me for a long time, I went back to bed feeling happy, preferring to know that he was thriving there rather than uncomfortable with me.

At the Prado, the second year, we split off at the entrance to see the galleries on our own. When I met up with him at the exit in the gardens, he was with a man, he'd gotten himself snatched up by a pedophile. I rushed at the man, scowling and growling at him like a wolf, the guy took off, Vincent asked what had gotten into me.

I gave the drugs back to the friend who had gotten them for me.

It was too cruel a contract: for us to see each other, he had to be sick *and* I had to be well.

Vincent didn't show up: it's not just being deprived of his body, but the collapse of expectations, that dream of travel, the primary perspective atrociously butchered, all at once. This morning, I'm like a casualty.

Holding on to a small amount of drugs when I spend the night with Vincent, even if I don't take them, provides me with a balancing pole that allows me to go right to the edge when I ravish his body.

I had a headache, I asked him to massage the trapezius muscles of my back. His coarse, shriveled palms, crazed by mycosis and detergent, passed gently over my shoulders; my heart made them as soft as silk.

He tells me he has a fantasy about watching a woman stick a vegetable in her vagina, adding, "And you, what's yours?" I can't do it.

Just when I thought I was incapable of writing anything, for the past two or three days I've been thinking about another book (it's always a joy to look forward to a new book): a faux travel diary, or a faux novel, a trip around the world in a Camper with Vincent and a gun, and maybe Vincent would become a woman in the story, would be named Jane? Like Jayne Mansfield.

I think that he said to me last time, "I would never be able to hurt you."

In those days I had very little money, but always a flask of expensive perfume. Before he left, he would order me to spread it on his torso until the last drop of it was gone.

I bless him every day for not having come here.

The others are sweet with me, but I'm not really there, I'm with the other who isn't there, I absent myself to find the absent one again. If he were there, I would undoubtedly be nowhere.

His ass is forbidden to me; he says it's made for caca.

I have the suspicion that he deliberately wrecked the end of our last evening together because he had already decided not to meet me here; he would have figured that my resentment would mitigate my grief. He won't come, but is cruel enough to offer me the amorous power of a sliver of hope.

I carried on tirelessly throughout the night, at one point I whispered to him, "Would you like me to lick your balls?" He replied, "I like everything," he was already asleep.

I listen to the music he gave me (reggae). I don't like it. It's a good exercise.

He says, "When you suck me off, in the light, I can see you have a bald spot, right there."

"When I come home at night, I strip down in front of the mirror, all day long I have to deal with my ugly face, but at least I have this, a beautiful torso, I especially like that one muscle, under my arm, do you like it too?"

The better part of the night with Vincent was spent trying to fuck me. It reminded me of those youthful sleepless nights, the very first ones, where sensuality takes precedence over exhaustion, where the vain search for pleasure becomes more exciting than the eagerly awaited-for pleasure, and where bodies start to give off a strange odor, beyond sexuality, a sweat of the absolute.

He has half-assed ideas: exporting underwater bicycles to Africa for deep-sea diving, becoming a porn star or stand-up comic, mounting a Club Med on an abandoned platform in the Congo.

Five days and five nights with Vincent in this strange city, five monotonous orgasms: he offers himself with inertia and resignation, I drench his thighs. I found no feeling of love for him until the moment I said goodbye, just after he disappeared.

Last night, slightly drunk, while looking at my right hand posed on the tablecloth, lit by the Christmas garlands peeking through the oleander, it seemed clear to me that that hand had only been created to be able to caress Vincent; this morning, that emotion became abusive.

He said, "Before I go, let's cuddle, would you rather I be on bottom or on top?"

When I saw Isabelle again, I confessed to her my plan that she pay back the debt of her betrayal by offering herself to the person I'm in love with, to Vincent, since he fantasizes about her. She asked me, "Is he handsome?" "No, he's a monster." "And does he love you?" My lips forced a burbled response, an onomatopoeia somewhere between "Bah!" and "Beuh!"

The honey soap he gave me is shrinking terribly fast; I only use it now on my genitals; together they give off a capital perfume.

He danced in my mouth.

He's barely arrived and starts begging me for a porno, when last time he had refused to watch one. I notice that he's wearing my black shirt with a white pattern; he adds, while unbuttoning the first button, "And your t-shirt." I bend down to look for a videotape with girls in it. When I get up, he's shirtless, sitting next to me on the couch. I find his skin again, splendid, clear of the little red dots from last month, marvelously soft and perfumed, with those beauty marks on his shoulders; I hardly dare to kiss it, I caress it shyly, as if I were getting it for the first time, I say to him, "You've given me a sacred present," and him, "It's true, my body isn't bad."

He danced to Prince's "Kiss" with his cock in my mouth; now I could ask him for anything.

When he drives me in his mother's car, he speeds, he skids, he slams on the brakes, he does 180s, he throws me around, I keep my mouth shut, I don't show that I'm happy.

He wants to take me boating with Max in the Bois de Boulogne, he says, "He's my best friend, I'm warning you, he doesn't know that we sleep together, there's nothing physical between us, ok? I hope you know how to behave." T. says they're going to knock me unconscious with the paddle.

After dinner, he asks me if the door to the bathroom has a lock on it; when he comes out, he shows me a line of brown powder sitting on top of the toilet, he says, "I laid it out for you, it's brown sugar, it's lower quality than the white, but it's cheaper." What was he doing all that time he was in there? When he leaves, he gives my cock a little kiss. He comes back, he's forgotten his heroin, I brush my teeth, he bites my ass. In bed, earlier, he did a pantomime of fucking me.

He begins to invoke shared memories, says, "We were really too adorable, that first night we spent together, in that hotel room in Agadir."

I stroked him so well, that isn't always the case, I was sure he was thinking: no one touches me like this.

He slept by my side, I always insist that he stay, this time I didn't insist, he nodded off in my arms while listening to music, just like before in front of the television while his bath was running, forgetting everything and the second I get my bearings I continue to suck and jerk him off, I guide his unconscious hand towards my prick, press it on top of it, by his fingers' involuntary movements I can tell he doesn't suspect that I've come, I fall asleep against him, suddenly wake up, get out at the end of the bed to turn off the lights, he undresses completely, stays on top of the covers, I ask him why he doesn't want to slide underneath, he says that he's sweating, later a coughing fit overtakes him, he escapes and sits up, the birds have begun to sing, it's five a.m., I tell Vincent about the Amazon, he goes to look out the window, pours himself a tall glass of vodka in the kitchen. When I wake up, hemmed in by the traces of that body I worshipped, that disappeared, I'm ready to rinse out my mouth with ammonia and powder the sheets and his pillow with sulphur.

When I see the vein that runs down my right arm, from this moment on I'll have the desire to pierce it, with him watching, with the bevelled tip of a syringe.

An episode that I had forgotten: I had known him for a little over a year, I had to attend the *Rencontres de la photographie d'Arles*, I had invited him to come with me, he couldn't, by chance I had given him the name of my hotel. One night, when I arrive at the screening, I find him standing at the theater gates. I'm so happy that I suddenly feel cold, tetanized by a joy that freezes me. He says, "I'm wrecked, I travelled all day hitchhiking to catch up with you, let's go to your hotel." I had only dreamed and dream of nothing but the moment I would find myself alone with him in my hotel room, and yet my lips drily reply, "We'll go later, let's go to the screening first." At the end of the screening, Vincent announces that he's leaving again; a burning misery follows an icy joy.

Because I saw him dance to that music, he reappeared in the empty space, suddenly dilated by that music.

I dream: Vincent sucks me off, finally, I get him to take my cock in his mouth, I notice that he has little white stars under his tongue, they must have escaped from the illuminated globe I left on to help me fall asleep.

A good trick for telephoning him when I'm anxious: put the music on really loud, and talk over it, it absorbs the anxiety.

He tells me about disgusting things: in the African restaurant where he spends his nights, most of the guys have AIDS; in the kitchen, they fuck these poor starving girls without wearing condoms, in exchange for frozen shark meat.

The time when I shaved a second time at night, just before seeing him, so I wouldn't scratch him.

He shows up in a poppy red nylon motorcycle suit, his head sticking ridiculously out of the top, and I burst out laughing, he says that if it's going to be like that he's leaving, I make him stay, he doesn't want to tell me what he did in the afternoon, he says that he won't admit it to anyone, that he's in heroin withdrawal, I ask him to show me his arms, he starts doing a striptease with the jumpsuit, peels it like a banana from top to bottom, reveals a white cotton undershirt with buttons on it that covers his whole body, now he claims to have been riding motorbikes all afternoon, he pushes away my hand, later in the night he takes his cock out of the jumpsuit, I had asked him to mess around, he lets me suck him off standing up while he watches cunts getting screwed on a video.

I gave him the lamp that he had admired, with its mixture of leather, ivory, and cobalt blue lacquered wood, I had bought it fifteen years ago with my first paycheck, along with the twenty dollars in gold that my grandmother left me when I was ten.

He was fifteen kilometers away, I was dancing with someone else, and yet I gave myself to the dance as if he were watching me, to impress him.

I am very early, the train is still empty; I decide, worn out from partying the night before, to rest a bit in the darkness, in my compartment. The ceiling lamp is lit, the window blind lowered, I want to turn out the light and lift the blind at the same time, but since these two gestures can't be performed simultaneously, at the end of a brief, half-conscious hesitation I raise the blind, just before turning out the light, and find myself several tens of centimeters away, separated only by the two windows of our parallel trains, from two boys sitting across from each other who are shooting up, whom I surprise and who surprise me in the light, but it's too sacred, too brutal and too crucial a moment to interrupt for a voyeur; my heart is racing, I'm terrified, and at the same time fascinated since it feels like I'm witnessing a performance (I've only seen that done in movies, and it always looks fake, like bloody noses; even if it's real, you don't ever believe it), more intimate than the sexual act, of an insane violence and complicity; I turned out the light the second they saw me, I lean back in the darkness, I observe them, I stare at them, it's an incredibly beautiful performance, of a beauty that makes me want to participate in it unconditionally, to project myself on the other side of the windows; there it is, they've found the vein, almost at the same moment, and throw the syringes on the floor, untie and fold up their arms, shake them, raise them up as if to make the substance move more quickly towards the heart, or towards the brain, they close their eyes, light a cigarette, don't give me another look; the boy I have the best view of if I'm sitting down starts to scratch the front of his neck, the nape, then lifts up his pant leg to scratch his shin; they no longer speak; the one closer to me straightens up and draws nearer, this time only a couple of centimeters away, to open the window, sits back down as he tastes the fresh air, then gets up to throw the syringes out the window, I'm afraid that he'll hurl them at me and hit my window but no, I no longer exist, he simply lets them fall down onto the rails, they're face to face once again in the compartment of the empty train, and I continue to bask in my contemplation; suddenly they return in the darkness to themselves; after a moment I can see the two red butts of their cigarettes rise and flutter around the light switch, which doesn't work; they go out into the corridor. I press my nose against the window so as to not lose sight of them, one sits down in the next compartment; when the light comes on, the other has gone further down the corridor; a conductor bolts down the dark hallway, chases them as if they were simple vagrants. When I come back, I tell Vincent the story, he says that it's filthy to shoot up.

1988   I surprise him at his shop; he's reading a book charred by a fire while scratching the soles of his feet.

We came together: was that the first time?

Vincent said to me, I have a fungus, he said, I have scabies, he said, I have a sore, he said, I have lice, and I pulled his body against mine.

In the bathroom of the hotel at Sables-d'Olonne, where, naked, he drew the water for our bath, I crouched behind him and started to suck his cock from underneath his ass, he said, "You really know how to do it, if you had tits I'd marry you in a minute." Later in the afternoon, stretched out 69 on one of the beds, I suck him while he jerks me off; I consider the scene, I ask him if I can photograph it from my point of view, his moist cock coming out of my mouth and his hand pulling on mine, he refuses, I come, he says that I made a horrible face.

From now on, in my datebook, out of superstition, I add a question mark after his first name.

I watch porn videos with girls in them sitting next to him, I caress his torso under his clothes, his hand protects his sex, after half an hour he takes it away, I rub his prick through his pants, without succeeding to unbutton them, I watch alongside him one of the images that moves me the most, a boy who licks a cock that moves in and out of a vagina, and he falls asleep.

This morning, under T. and C.'s sheets, I jerk off while inventing an eternal scenario: I'm allowed to lick

Vincent, but not to suck him off, we've decided on it together; every time I try, despite this prohibition, he can beat me until I bleed.

Ever since I spent a holiday with him (Christmas night, last year), every new holiday makes him present to me.

By a strange stroke of luck, while taking a look I never should have taken through the inside of the sleeve of a record I don't listen to anymore, I had found the thin and scintillating mica, licorice-colored, of the opium that made us so high together two years ago, and that I thought he had stolen. A new ritual gives me access to his body while he prepares a glass of ice water, wraps it up in a piece of aluminum foil pierced with little holes, held together with an elastic, on top of which he collects a pile of cigarette ash to help the sputtering bullet to burn; but the charm has evaporated from the stuff.

Another evening with Vincent, one of the last? He gives me a present for my birthday, a small painted comb and a honey soap; by chance I salvaged the wrapping paper that he had let me throw out without telling me about the note that accompanied it; I read it and melt, it's so affectionate; afterwards, he makes a great effort to take it back from me and put it in his wallet.

Now he wants to introduce me to his brother, the one I haven't met; he says that we look like each other.

He reread my book, *Voyage avec deux enfants*, he said that it showed him how disgraceful his character is.

I keep the night inside me for hours and hours, for days, before recounting it. Like so often, what preserves it is an image: late into the night, sitting on my bed, I hold him up as he's lying in my arms, almost unconscious, his eyes closed, one arm behind his shoulders holding the nape of his neck, the other threaded under his thighs, my caresses have lifted his undershirt up to his neck, I haven't removed his boxers; having exhausted the connection between my palm and his torso, I can only access his body in this figure drawn from the Pietà through the brush of my lips, sometimes touching his nipple, sometimes touching his lips eaten away by herpes, sometimes touching the tip of his sex, a bit of saliva on his breast wakes him (heroin + hashish).

He showed up two hours late. I throw him on the bed by grabbing and tackling him; I wedge his head under my elbow, pull his hair, pinch the cartilage of his nose really hard, twist his fingers, push his eyes back into his head, slip a hand underneath his clothes to taste the warmth of his skin.

When will I be rid of him, the pathetic little shit?

He must be afraid to face me: stage fright of becoming my character again.

I'm waiting for the person who could share my life with me, these next two years, and who without a doubt won't share it.

Dream: a gang of them arrives in the house, but the heat doesn't work, most are about to leave when Vincent says very lightly, "We'll sort it out," which I interpret as, "I'm staying here with you." My entire night pivots on these soft words.

(How I love Vincent: ready to open up my chest to lay my heart at his feet.)

Like a luminous fish, he who glowed all night goes out in the end, to escape my caresses; I offer my lips to a black hole.

I had wanted to slip so many skins on Vincent: that of a whore, that of a child, that of a thug, that of a sadist, that of just anyone.

I love Vincent, that's the problem, and my actual solitude? Bernard says that it's impossible to share having a mad crush on someone.

He takes me to his dealer, he goes to get money from an ATM and I put in the other half, we walk up to the fifth floor, the guy's in front of the TV in the middle of eating a hamburger that he had delivered, there's another guy there who's rather handsome, thin, all in black, whom I saw arrive on a motorcycle while I was waiting for Vincent in the car; it's ten-thirty, the dealer can't find the little piece of white paper with the powder in it, he remembers having shown it to his friend but now he doesn't know where he hid it, he turns the place upside down, gets annoyed, his friend tells him not to think about it, to keep eating, to watch TV, to think about something else and it will come back to him, but it doesn't come back to him, he calls Vincent into the hallway to ask him if I'm a narc.

Vincent splendid, elegant, tender, funny: calls me my Guibert and strokes my ear, gives me little kisses. At the end of the night, he takes off after refusing to sleep with me, says that the Bible condemns homosexuality, adds that I was only able to rape him all those times because he was dead drunk.

Looking at the unmade-up, slightly downy cheek of that beautiful young woman, I could feel the skin that I like to kiss on Vincent's cheeks.

Went to see Vincent at his job in the Métro, several hours before his departure for Portugal, where he didn't want to take me. He talks about my self-esteem; I find him hideous.

I called him, I had decided to ask him the question, "Would you agree to prostitute yourself for me? Four hundred bucks for half an hour, I'll lick you." That isn't true, I didn't dare.

He says, while smoking his joint, that he sat on the candy seller's face, and that she licked his ass. He says, while turning up the volume of the music, "It isn't that late." I say, "Anyway, the neighbors aren't home, you could thrash me, no one would hear a thing."

Vincent arrives an hour late, he says, "I made a new perfume cocktail for you, vanilla-nutmeg," and he unbuttons his shirt to make me smell it; I kiss his breast.

Last night, Vincent's cock tasted like fresh paper in the books from the *Bibliothèque Verte*.[1]

Suddenly, in the middle of the party, maybe because of the drugs, it seemed clear to me that Vincent was my assassin, that I only went out with him for that, and that he would finish me off tonight, absurdly, without drama, in that depressing banality.

Vincent in front of me, not the slightest attraction to him, he has bare feet, it's been so long since I could suck on them for hours (I mention this, and he has no memory of it); even kissing them with the tips of my lips would be unusual.

---

1. A popular French series of children's books.

He did a moving job the night before and arrives exhausted, he had trouble climbing my five flights of stairs, he asks me to massage his calves with an ointment; this time, there's something pitiful about the scene, but it pleases me all the same.

He was naked beside me but I was so drunk that my memory retained nothing of that nudity: as if he hadn't been naked, as if he hadn't been there.

I adore this: in bed, he makes a real scene, he claims that I'm assaulting him, that more than once I've bruised his nipples while caressing them. He is afraid to entrust his cock to my mouth, afraid that a stroke of madness will make me devour it.

It's no longer Buster Keaton, it's Boris Karloff: when I see him arrive with that scar on his forehead, the black, bulging eye, his hair slicked back in a cowlick, I'm seized by a terror that verges on an uncontrollable fit of laughter.

He leaves, I stagger, I go to pick up some drugs that I dropped by mistake, I pick up cum in my fingers.

This evening with Vincent, something new: I vomited.

If I weren't fixated on Vincent, I would want the whole world: an uninterrupted hiccup of concupiscence, a ragged stare.

I took out his photo again, I looked him in the eyes for a long time, once again enchanted by the detail of the beauty mark on the left side of his torso (I had borrowed T.'s Leica: did I focus on the eye, or the nipple?). As night fell, there was nothing left to do but take a photo of the photo, posed as if on an altar, illuminated by the three miniature lamps I bought in a scale model shop. The photo of the photo: a way to lose a bit of the print's precision, to pull away from its false presence.

Writing about him is an appeasement.

(53)

Torpor upon returning home: stifling heat, the oppressive void of the holidays, and an obsession that grows larger, like an absurd, giant marionette: Vincent's cock, soft and swallowed up, aqueous, dust.

Always happy to discover his face, his droopy eyelid and lazy eye, his narrow, fleshy mouth crazed by tobacco, there where I'm least expecting it: in the portrait of Horst by Bérard, amidst the pages of an album I'm flipping through, in these photos of Buster Keaton scattered through his memoirs that I'm reading to get away from Faulkner's dark complications.

While they're away, I go into his parents' living room for the first time, and find, arranged on a cabinet, photographs of children: three boys and a girl. A large photo in black and white of Vincent when he was very young, with an astonishing smile (that he still has), hidden by smaller photos of the three others; among them, a splendid young boy, the older brother whom I've never seen. "I don't want you to meet him," Vincent says when he sees me pick up the photo, "Because he would also like to meet you." The Rover we rented is waiting downstairs; we leave the apartment.

If I stay with him, it's also because he's the only one who allows me to maintain a link with my youth; its illusion manifests in bursts, accelerations, excesses.

The next morning, across from the cozy bed in which I had finally found a good night's sleep, after so long, as if sleep had been made possible by the irradiation of his body next to mine, the ugly painting was still off the wall, and we had to put it back before we left the room: Vincent, as if he were giving me a last little gift, climbed up on the chair and exaggerated the strain of rehanging the painting, leaving me just enough time to undo his pants to kiss his little white cheeks, so deliciously firm, contracted by the threat of my tongue that was longing for the hole.

Finally I meet up with him; we exchange a few cold words; he doesn't come; I suddenly lose my erection. A little over a month ago, we shared a bath; he stood up as he was getting hard, his cock covered in suds, I sucked it until it recovered its actual taste... I need only to think of this: exactly one year ago, I would have never imagined that barely six months later, Christmas night, we'd be dancing waltzes together at the London Club, drunk and in each other's arms, shoving our tongues in each others' mouths. Nothing I had dreamt of then could ever be blissful as that reality to come. Perhaps many such ecstasies await me still?

To think of him as a rent boy, that's what I need to do.

Every time I call him, I humiliate myself. Tried just now to jerk off violently while sucking my thumb, to make myself think of his little cock, but it didn't make me think of anything.

I would have liked to photograph his prick surrounded by fragrant, pale pink peonies: I would have loved that splash of blood at the moment of stabbing him, to feel disgusted and pleased when those warm pieces of his brain hit me just as I shatter his skull; yes, I would really love to touch his brain.

Heard the trace of a guilty conscience in his voice for the first time when he called to cancel on me: the first sign of a break-up. I cross myself straightaway. Memory of the day I hadn't even been glad to make him cry.

Seeing Vincent at night is a joy from the moment I wake up, from the night before, from the morning of the night before, from the night of the day before the night before; last time, he canceled at the last minute.

Vincent at the hospital: in good shape, he sleeps for two days, sobers up, "recovers." He seems happy to see me. I open the closet door so no one can see us through the open door, and I tear away the sheet, I force his prick out of his jogging pants and the pink boxers I gave him, I try to suck it, he struggles, I slap him around. Five minutes later, I cross his parents in the hallway, they look younger than I had thought they were by the sound of their voices; they stare at me with respect, as if I were their son's patron.

With him, I lose all dignity; isn't that why I cling so intensely to him?

The missing person in my life: the one who would know how to beat me; I believed at one time that he would come out of T., that there would be another being inside him that would split off, but that didn't happen; I thought for a long time that he would be Vincent, but that didn't happen either. Sometimes I dread the necessity of writing it down like this, but writing immediately makes the tortures it declares collapse: the unspeakable.

I returned to the antique dealer's window; the sought-after painting had disappeared; renting the Rover with Vincent had cost exactly the same price as the painting.

He hadn't brought any drugs for our trip, only a bottle of perfume made from wildflowers, so that the softness of our skin would become a substitute joy and hallucination. Fell asleep easily by his side, dropping off against him while he was watching television; the small, ordinary joy of others becomes my great, exceptional joy.

I spent the afternoon stretching out my asshole with a dildo so that he could enter me easily; when he telephoned

I was in the middle of deburring it of shit and lubricating it; I had planned on spending the evening with him with the dildo in my ass, without telling him, dancing around the moment when I would decide to confess.

At seven, from work, Vincent cancels on me. Whether he's telling me the truth ("I don't feel well," "I feel tired even though I shouldn't be," "I have a sore throat,") or lying, it's undeniable that he would prefer not to see me tonight, and there's nothing more to say about that.

Evening with Vincent, a disaster. Both of us furiously attempt to avenge ourselves of this feeling, he takes a condom out of his wallet and tries to fuck me, while I want him to so much, I can't manage to let him in, he tells me he doesn't fuck virgins. I suck him off for a long time, until he falls asleep. At four in the morning, he has diarrhea, and leaves.

I turn on all the lights, I wait for Vincent, I think again of suicide.

Sunday, nine a.m., silence and solitude; I still have stomach pains; as soon as I wake up, I do things to prepare for his arrival at night: I turn on the radiator in the bedroom, while I usually leave it off, so I don't have to think about turning it on again, since I'll turn off the heating system when I leave to have lunch with my great-aunts, and an automatic timer will turn the whole thing on again towards evening, so my room won't be too overheated or too cold, but that its temperature will make him want to undress; I don't give a second thought to wearing my favorite underwear, even though the pressure of the elastic on my herpes zoster will murder me all day; nine a.m., he's sleeping, he partied all night, I know how he sleeps, I know the position of his hand, folded on top of his torso, I know every inch of his body, better than the person who might actually be sleeping next to him, I want to be unbeatable on that body; tonight he'll come back into my field of vision and within reach of my hand; his hand gave me my last orgasm, it's been over fifteen days now because he's been sick; I'm tempted to make a vow that from now on only his hand will be permitted to appease me; again I think about what Sophie told me about her relationship with Benoit; to get her to beat him, he started beating her; the abandon caused by the enslavement he imposed on her first made him repugnant to her, then bound him to her in an extraordinary way, overwhelmed by the image of a defenseless soul, shackled by its ghosts.

How all these episodes with Vincent in this journal have something ordinary about them, the paltry rendered precious.

Strange evening: I'm doubled over with stomach cramps; I had decided to eat alone at the vegetarian place, and then to see *Andrei Rublev* again; Vincent calls me around seven o'clock, saying that his chick stood him up; an evening with Vincent can't be refused; I wait for him without drinking in a communal warmth that's perhaps superior to that of drunkenness, without feeling anxious; he calls me at eight o'clock saying that his car has broken down three hundred meters from his house, and that I'd better believe him because he's in a rage, a sweat, exhausted, he's waiting for a friend to come and tow the car; I cheerfully wish him good luck and set out on the evening I had originally planned.

Vincent is unavailable: he must just have gotten his paycheck, and prefers to spend it without me, with girls, the punk.

Reread with emotion, while waiting for Vincent last night, *Fragments of a Lover's Discourse*: feeling that I often pursue the things that Barthes indicates.

Nine-twenty, it's beautiful out, I start to work; I drank a bit too much vodka last night, I should never drink alcohol; Vincent looked gray, glassy-eyed; he attracts me even if he looks terrible, he was so spectacular three days ago; with the money Bernard gave him for the work he did on his house he had bought himself a jogging suit with two colored stripes running down his chest; after dinner, I pull down the waistband to deep-throat him, I watch as I do it, I lick his little wrinkled balls, he tells me that I'm crazy tonight, he jerks me off and makes me come, says that now he knows how to make me come, and that my orgasm is such a big fuss, I cried out, he doesn't want me to make him come, says that he's impotent.

Yes, the waiting is delicious; getting drunk while waiting is delicious (I am, as always in writing, at once the scientist and the rat he disembowels for research).

There will be a ray of light under the door; I watch for it, and I watch for the steps that pass by my landing, temporarily erasing my anxiety; there will be the tapping of his fingers against the door or, if the music is too loud, a very short ring of the doorbell; this waiting makes me suffer slightly, I love this waiting; these days, I don't wait for him anymore to start drinking, so I don't look too grim when he arrives.

He's coming over; changing clothes three times; being in love.

Dissatisfaction, patience: even so, an insane solitude at night, around six-thirty, when I'm not sure that Vincent will call, and before the first glass of wine; I worked all day, well enough I think; in short, I am rather unhappy.

Vincent came by to install a dimmer for me, to complete the work of the young electrician who died: he climbed up on a chair, rose up on the tips of his toes to reach the wires on the ceiling that still had to be cut, the chair is rickety, I hold on to him by his thighs, once again I feel something pictorial in the loose grip of my hands on either side of his blue pants, the tan leather inlay of his belt, the skin of his back that the slightest movement risks baring, and my lips holding back a kiss (often, this impression, in erotic situations, of painting certain postures, transparent tableaus).

"Calm yourself," Vincent tells me, at that apogee.

On the blade of the knife, more than a week later, still a touch of that powder that gave me such bliss with Vincent.

When I no longer feel in love with Vincent, I have the feeling that something has closed down in my life.

Not such a great evening with Vincent. I should have respected the cadence that he indicates, casually, for our relationship: "from time to time" (I complain that I can't ever call him, and that he never calls me: "I do, he replies, "but only from time to time.") He's in bad shape, he seems worn out by his work, he says that he'll quit at the end of six months so he can collect unemployment. I take him to an unbearable restaurant. He comes back to my place, as if to keep me from feeling left out, but he says he won't stay long, he has to sleep. I take off his four layers of sweaters and t-shirts one by one, he keeps his black pants on, he is bare-chested, I love his body very much at that moment, it has gotten some of its fleshiness back. We fight. When he wants to leave, I jerk off violently at his feet, he tells me to make sure I don't soil his pants; I continue to suck him off while I feel his four layers of clothes brush up against my face one after the other, he's getting dressed again; in my right hand, I hold the belt he had tried to whip me with at the end of my arm, bent and outstretched towards him; he doesn't take it from me right away; I delight in the pictorial blindness I feel in our suspension, which will quickly undo itself at the moment when my pleasure will make me want to lift my head towards his face. He puts his belt back on, it's true that I would have liked him to beat me with it, but with my downstairs neighbors it's a bit awkward; we would have to go to a hotel to beat each other (here again, the character of a novel insinuates itself in me).

I always tell myself: I won't call him, and then I call, too soon after our last encounter. I'm afraid of getting his boss, I try to adopt a neutral, confident tone, but when I do get the boss my voice breaks in the middle of his name and the way he says "Hold on" leads me to think that he knows I'm a lover, that I'm a joke. I know that my manner of speaking, my speed, my confidence will be decisive, he'll make me pay for it for sure, he'll make me pay for that intonation of emotion. I know that to say, "We'll see each other tonight," up front, and with an exclamation point rather than a question mark, gives me more of a chance than "Are you free tonight?" In surprise, there's always a moment of hesitation; he knows that I know that it contains the possibility of his resorting to a lie, and that if he says no to me it isn't necessarily that he isn't free, but that he has decided as much, that he detected a hint of pathos in my voice, and doesn't want to come to its rescue; he only says yes when we share a common prescription; he is always the diagnostician of our relationship.

I wake up early; my watch, that's worked since my first communion, won't stop stopping, insidiously; I think, he must be getting up, like he told me, his father or mother are yelling from behind the door for him to hurry up; a little later, I think, he's arrived at the shop, he's weighing the sachets of herbs, he's making a delivery; I rush to call him, I'm afraid of reaching his boss.

We had planned on the young electrician coming back to finish installing the low-voltage lighting system in my entranceway: the wires are exposed, and several holes had been carelessly left in the ceiling. I think the system is a little too sophisticated (I was ashamed to admit how much it cost to the young electrician, who asked about it), I look at those unsightly wires, and think: he left it like that a week ago, he needs to fix it; his mother found him dead in his bed on Saturday morning. I will ask Vincent to finish the work.

Vincent was in the middle of shitting, and I tried to suck him off: it wasn't depravity or the search for an exceptional thrill, it was simply a movement of love.

As if poisoned by this happiness: impossible for it to permeate everyday life, not to want to recreate it; to see it, him, again!

He caressed me, he said, "If I stayed, I would draw you while you were sleeping," and he rested his head in the hollow of my chest.

If he would at least let me lavish him with the love I am capable of, I could stay alive and well in this world!

I must be able to document that moment, for it was immense, but its *récit* would also have to be as crystalline as a Cavafy poem: the impalpable and sacred monument of human love. Some day, at some time, that character drowned in his love, he felt his heart beat in the chest of the other he held against him, his body no longer belonged to him, he was an offering, and the other had the kindness to ensure that he didn't drown in the waves, to hold him softly afloat between his arms and the great eternity (cocaine on top of weed from the Congo).

"What's it about?" asks Vincent's mother; urge to respond, "It's about his cock, Madame, I need to suck it as soon as possible."

Melancholy Vincent: despite Pierre's urgings, he wouldn't sleep with him when he was in Paris; to get back at him, Pierre screwed his girlfriend. We do cocaine; as Vincent points out, "It's not very sensual," I haven't the slightest interest in his cock, which I love so much. My eye nearly touching his closed eyelid, I remember all the times I felt happy lying next to him.

I started to suck him off, he said, "Doesn't it bother you? It was in Flo's pussy this morning, and I haven't washed it."

I passed my hand underneath his ass to hold his cock, and he said, "That's how my aikido professor used to suck me off."

While drunk: I miss Vincent, his little prick, his little smile.

Evening with Vincent: we jerk off, we laugh.

I think I'm not in love with Vincent any more, I don't call him. But I look in the window at Zorro to see if he's there.

Feeling of having lost a fiancé, a character: Vincent.

1987   Vincent: the squalor of his face, his clothes, his life. Studies up on the crystal and porcelain business at night, wakes up at seven a.m. to follow his cold-calling sales route, goes door-to-door in the afternoon, gets drunk in the evening on beer and mezcal at Zorro, a dive bar in the Bastille.

Christmas night, heroin and alcohol, I dance with Vincent cheek to cheek.

Vincent says to me, when I pay the check—with rare venison steak in our bellies—"Three hundred fifty francs to have dinner with me, you must either love me, or be rich, or have no sense of money at all." He pockets the check for his mother.

While jerking me off, Vincent makes me fantasize aloud about women I've never had. Of course, he fantasizes about my sister, makes me describe her, asks to meet her, and I deliver.

Forgot to note, in the episode of Vincent in tears, the most important thing: while walking with him at the end of the Champs-Elysées, without turning towards him, within the certitude of no longer loving him, I'm suddenly overtaken by an extraordinary surge of love that makes me take him in my arms, without daring to look at him, and hold him tight. But right then I have the impression that what I'm holding on to has no consistency; it isn't, assuredly, someone other than Vincent that I'm holding in my arms, it isn't even myself, but rather the symbol or phantom of love that I had for Vincent, so wasted that I can no longer control it, that it melts in my arms while thinking it holds itself up.

The other day, when calling Vincent, I reach his mother, she says: "Is this Hervé? May I ask you a question?" (I shudder in anticipation) "Is the H in your name an aspirated H?" I reply that I have no idea. She asks, "Do they say *mon beau Hervé*, or *mon bel Hervé*?" While I'm speechless, she adds, "You know, we wanted to name Vincent's brother Hervé, we even called him Hervé for three days, but we weren't sure about this aspirated H problem, and so in the end we named him Gregory, but now I regret it... Ok, I'll hand you to Vincent."

It was decided that I would have dinner last night with Vincent at Bernard's, and that we would stay and sleep together there, on the fold-out couch in front of the fire. Vincent shows up at eleven-thirty with a pathetic story to explain why he was late. All of a sudden I see him as Bernard must see him: the eyes of love obscure reality.

We very quickly separate: I no longer want to go with him to the isle of Elba.

Atrociously in love? Is love not a pretext for despair?

Vincent touches his tongue to my lips, then, just barely, to my tongue: nothing but that, nothing more, a stunning moment.

The other night, one of the first nights of really bitter cold, we had a date at seven in front of the cinema Saint-Germain to see *Mauvais Sang*. I drink a tea at the café counter, I notice him behind the window, sitting on a bench, he finally sees me, gets up, he's wearing a vest with a fur collar, his skateboard in his hand. He seems fairly awake. He tells me that he has forgotten everything about the other night, and asks me to describe for him the film that we had seen together several days earlier, *Down by Law*. I am glad to be seeing this film with him that T. had wanted to see with me: the parachute jump, the mad dash over the Bowie song, the dead ventriloquist who speaks... Happiness. We have dinner at the Vietnamese place on rue Princesse. He tells me he has to go to a party, I ask him to spend some time with me at my place anyway, we take off our clothes and go to bed, he tells me not to touch his sex, but that he'll jerk me off, on the condition that I don't look at him, I close my eyes, then sneak them open: his outstretched palm, several millimeters away from my eyelids without touching them, obscures them; at one point, I'm not sure if it was with his lips or his tongue, but just for one second, I feel him taste my prick. I come while saying to him, "I'm not allowed to look at you, but you can look at me?" When he leaves, he kneels down to rub my cock against the fur collar of his vest, he tells me that he stole it from Florence, and that from now on, without knowing it, she'll be buried in the scent of my prick.

I've fallen so behind in this notebook that now I have to recount two evenings with Vincent, each of which is a bit opposed to the other. For the several days that preceded the first, I couldn't stop thinking about how to help him, I even consulted Hedi, the psychiatrist who had signed his certificate for the army, and we came to the conclusion that there's nothing to be done. When the day arrived, finding him devastated by who knows what drug, dressed like a little pimp, in a daze at the movie theatre and asking me questions as if he were seven years old, then going on and on in the restaurant, unable to touch the food he ordered thinking he was hungry, I dump him on the Champs-Elysées at Franklin-Roosevelt station, and continue walking to take the Métro at Clemenceau. He pops up at a cross-point in the hallway, tells me that we can't leave each other like that. While I was walking, I had thought I would never see Vincent again, and that each step between the two stations was lowering an iron curtain between us by a notch. I tell him that I accept that our relationship is a disaster, but that it surpasses an acceptable minimum. Our backs are against either side of the tunnel, groups of commuters are passing between us. Vincent leaves again. I suddenly have the desire to be kind. I go looking for him: there are three corridors to choose from, he isn't in the first two, I find him walking in front of me in the third, I wondered if he recognizes my gait, he doesn't turn around, I say to him: "Vincent?" and find his face covered in tears.

Feeling cheerful one morning, I return to the shop I keep returning to, so I can take a look at that painting I love so much, of the young boy with the sullen face, dressed in black—who makes me think of Vincent—sketched in mesmerizing chalk lines, stretched out on the grim, bare floor. For several days now, having walked past the window, I've known that the painting has disappeared. But my good mood makes me think that I can face disappointment headlong, overcome it, and I go into the shop. The dealer isn't there, instead a woman is there whom I've never seen. I start by asking the price of a different painting, and if I may go into the back room of the shop, which is really just a narrow corridor with overcrowded walls. I immediately notice a very large painting, the largest, on the floor facing the wall, the only one that's turned around. I wait until the woman's back is turned to gently lift it away from the wall, and it's the one: a small red dot is affixed to the corner, which I immediately slide into my pocket. I flag down the saleswoman: "And this one, how much is it?" —"Oh, that one is already sold." I ask, "To another dealer?" "No, it just went to a stranger... Why? Do you like it?" I leave the shop totally devastated.

Such a desire to see Vincent dance (I'm drunk), dance on his waves.

Yesterday evening with Vincent. He adds vodka to his champagne, he says that he's taking antibiotics, he's exhausted, and plus he has something nasty, that thing

on the bottom of his feet that he hid from me the other
time; he went to see a dermatologist in the neighbor-
hood, it's a fungus that he waited too long to take care
of, I shouldn't touch it, it isn't really contagious, but it
would be better to be careful. He asks me if I want to
see his sores, I say yes, he takes off his shoes, he says,
"Do you want to see the more disgusting foot, or the
other one?" I reply, "The more disgusting one." He
takes off his sock, grips his foot to show me the arch,
studded with little red marks, glistening with ointment.
Then he turns around and takes off his sweater to show
me this patch he has in the middle of his back. He says
that if it's AIDS, he'll rob a bank, or maybe he'll shoot
himself during the hold-up, or else he'll take the money
and blow it all. We go out to dinner. He takes me back
home, he doesn't want to come up, he has an early
appointment with a tax guy for a part-time job in the
month of September, he wants to be in good shape for
it, I insist that he come up anyway, even if it's only for
five minutes, he kindly agrees, says that I'm a kamikaze.
On my bed, he curls up against me in my arms, I stroke
his torso a little, he's all warm. In the morning, I wake
up with a feeling of deep disgust. I change all the
sheets. I spray myself with anti-fungal powder. I make
an appointment with the dermatologist in the afternoon, I lie to him, I say that by accident I slept with a
young man whom I'll definitely never see again, whom
I have no way of contacting, and I describe Vincent's

sores, he assures me that no fungus in the world ever took a form like that.

Vincent refuses my help: will I ever get angry with him? I tremble with sadness. With this very sad fact: that I love most the one who humiliates me the most. To reach a very real masochism—is it more bearable than masochism in the abstract?

Evening with Vincent. He arrives looking dashing. I tell him about my last affair, show him pictures of the boy, I see something new in his eyes, he's a little jealous, he says that the boy looks like a little jerk. He tells me tales about his girlfriends. He has to go for his military service evaluation the day after tomorrow; he has stopped shaving. Going down the stairs, he turns around ever so slightly and asks, "So, are we going on this trip together?" I tell him we'll talk about it at dinner. I take him to the Brazilian restaurant where I should have taken him the last time, the night that was such a failure. We talk for a bit about that night, even though I had decided not to; I tell him that I was no doubt the one who made it go wrong, half-unconsciously, so that we'd so stupidly break up; later I confess that T. had devised a plan to surprise us so he could have sex with us, and that's what I was trying to avoid, thereby providing him, with my skewed reasoning, a reason to dump me. Suddenly, he falls apart: he says that he's been putting on an act for all his friends, that he's never felt so awful. For the first time, he realized his parents were idiots. He reproached them (for not being independent at twenty, for not earning his own living) and then, before they left, to make themselves feel better, they got drunk with him. Then they left for a month on vacation without leaving him anything, neither money nor food. He wrote bad checks, the banker telephoned to threaten him, said that the bank would confiscate his checking account for good and file charges against him. He's barely eaten anything for a week, he sleeps all the time, and he's too starved to ingest the food that's put in front of him, it disgusts him. He is pallid, almost grey, now beyond ugly, his teeth are covered with white and yellow filaments, he shivers with fear, and this is the person I love, whom I have loved. I feel like I'm my father sitting across from me. I immediately try to resurrect Michel within myself to replace him, his surety, his sense of fairness. My dead friend speaks through my mouth to comfort Vincent, to chase away his panic. I ask Vincent what he wants to do, he responds: "Sleep." I say, "At your place or my place?" He says, "I'll sleep at your place." He gets in bed before me, I ask him which way he wants to feel me in bed, half-dressed or naked, and he uncovers the sheet to show me that he is naked, I undress and get in bed next to him, I ask him: "Touching or no touching?—I'm very wary of taking advantage of his weakness—he replies, "No touching," puts out the light, and places his hand powerfully on the top of my torso, his hand warms me and gives me the impression of love. I don't move. During the night, the idea of traveling with him panics me. In the morning, he's more cheerful. I caress him very slowly, his torso, his shoulders, his arms, his stomach, and when the sheet moves I can tell that he is hard. We fight: I want to take his cock in my mouth. I finally swallow it, and he lets me and holds it for me so I can suck it better, and when I let it go our eyes meet. When I see him lift up one of his feet in the shower, it looks from a distance like the arch of his foot is stained red. I remember that the doctor had asked me to show him the bottoms of my feet when we had talked about AIDS. Vincent is sitting on the bed, I tell him, "Show me your feet," he refuses, he says, "I'm hiding something from you." I say, "What?" He says, "I have AIDS." I say that at least it's a good way to get exempt from service. He says, "You think?" When we're leaving, I give him a check to cover his overdraft. We leave to have breakfast together. It's pretty upbeat; I feel like we're good together. In the afternoon, he telephones and we decide to cancel that trip to the Atlantic coast.

Bolstered by my relationship with that other young man, I call Vincent, delivered of the evil spell that makes me approach him in a way from which he can only withdraw.

Vincent arrives completely stoned, more attractive than ever. We go to dinner. Then he dumps me in front of my apartment. T. comes over to pick up the pieces.

Last night I do with Vincent practically everything I do with T.: he kisses me, I suck him off, he puts on a condom to fuck me, we put on cock rings, we sniff poppers, he whips me (but all of this is done shyly, as if we were children at play)... For the first time in four years, his tongue approaches my lips and carefully opens up my mouth: this could prove to be the advent of one of the greatest dreams of my life, and of course, ennui prowls around us.

Vincent should be coming over in less than an hour to spend the night with me, and yet I feel desperate.

Vincent's friend, the other Vincent, crashed his car into a wall and botched his suicide attempt. Vincent is putting him up when he gets out of the hospital: would I rather be that survivor?

Tried the other night, when faced with him at Bernard's opening, to abandon my feelings for Vincent.

Trip with Vincent. I take these notes, in the car, while we're smoking, on the little blue receipt from the bank:

Hymn to the rain.

Hymn to fabric (I had just felt his thigh through his pants)

Hymn to delicacy.

Invention of love.

The (one) task of literature: to learn to keep quiet.

Vincent takes his eyes away from the road to try to see what I'm writing on the ticket.

The first time I saw Vincent again: a spate of gleeful fighting before dinner—something we've discovered both of us enjoy—afterwards, he comes back to my place, he says: "I'll make you two propositions: a magnetic massage, or else I'll sodomize you." For half an hour, I don't respond, so I can continue to play with him. When he asks me the question again, I say to him: "The magnetic massage."

I take ecstasy with T. again, that vile white powder, and it's not the unparalleled bliss I found with Vincent: it's an abyss, a demolition of the entire construction of my life and my consciousness, an effacement of identity, on the threshold of madness. It's also the death of my relationship with Vincent, since it's the death of my relationship with drugs, and I know that my relationship with Vincent can only exist through drugs. To counter such a cruel and stupid prophecy, I call Vincent, I tell him simply that I would like to see him, he's available, he comes over, we talk, we listen to music (the new Etienne Daho record, a good sentimental omen), we drink some champagne, then go have dinner at Tchaika, Vincent has his mom's car, I love driving through the city with him at the wheel, we drink a lot of bison grass vodka, I gave him my book with a dedication and the prints I had made of his photographs, I let him take them with him when we left my apartment to give him the freedom to choose not to come back, when leaving the restaurant I ask him to take me back

(83)

home in the car, it's parked pretty far away, for several hundred meters we follow a trail of drops of wet blood that forms a puddle in places, Vincent said that it must be a prank, that at that distance the guy would already have bled out, he crouches down to examine a spot and says with a laugh that his heart just jumped, the trail stops just in front of the car, underneath a broken window. Back at my apartment, before we stop the car, I ask Vincent if he'd rather come up and finish the champagne or go back to his house, he says playfully, "Finish the champagne"; once inside, I strip down in front of him completely, lie down on my bed and tell him to do the same, he's blown away, he doesn't object, and here he finally is in my bed, almost naked (he kept his underwear on) beside me, I get hard, I feel good, happy, I caress him, I lick and suck his nipples, I ask him to caress me, he starts working on my ear, he says that he really likes ears, I clench him in my arms, I rub my prick in soft, even movements against his thigh, I jerk him off at the same time, he gets really hard, I feel the down on his cheeks against my lips, oh! how I adore him, I recite that exercise of adoration I am always capable of with him, I kiss his prick for a long time before sucking it, then I swallow it all at once, it is so good, so sweet, so little, so brave, so splendid, so very deliciously, lightly scented, Vincent says that he rarely eats pussy because the smell is too strong, I say that maybe he can sodomize me one day with a condom, he says, "Are you afraid of AIDS?" I tell him, "You fucked so many little negresses in Africa," he says, "You'd like that, I'm sure, little black girls with sugary skin, nice and hot," I tell him perhaps he will love me one day, he says, "Yes, perhaps." He's getting ready to go to the Libyan or Iranian border to put up hospital beds in the war zones. Salary: 15,000 francs a month (which is about what I make at the newspaper), and double that in the more dangerous zones. We plan on taking a trip together, to Portugal, to Lisbon. On this beautiful first day of May, a radioactive cloud flies over Europe.

While going through my contact sheets looking for photos to put together a birthday album for T. (I'm already really late with it), I come across several photos of Vincent that I never printed. I struggle with the mystery of the violence of this love—the photographs remind me strongly of this—and I tell myself that I would like to describe it with the solemnity of the sacred, as if it were one of the great religious mysteries. The tongues of flame, for example, that fall on the apostles. Last night, while going to bed, agonizing, I get up to find a print I had just had made of one of the photos, I look at it while laying back on my bed, holding it at the end of my arm, bringing it closer, extending it out; I don't have too many sexual thoughts, of fucking or of defilement, violent hallucinations that would bring sex or lechery into play, but rather the suspended grace of bearing witness to a transfiguration.

Discovered Vincent thanks to a touch of shared white powder, vile to the tongue (ecstasy): found his eyes, his lips, his navel, our fidelity, our affection. A beautiful moment.

1986   Hyperrealistic dream of a suddenly consensual Vincent that gives me the insane idea today to call him? To think of going on another trip with him? To kill myself with him?

Another catastrophic evening with Vincent. Still mad with desire for him. He arrives at seven and says he has to leave again at nine. He talks about ass for an hour, takes off his pants to show me his long underwear that protects against the cold. I spend an hour trying to get him into bed and then he bitches that I'm the only one of his friends who wants to touch him like that, undress him, suck him off. He threatens to knock me unconscious with the telephone and steal the cocaine I had wanted to do with him. He leaves, calling me a whore.

Vincent wakes up early to make sandwiches. So far from his ways. Reminder of the harshness of life, at one point where I'm threatened by, or threaten to, break it off.

I notice, while flipping through an album, that I also loved Vincent because he looked like Buster Keaton.

Obsession (always Vincent's cock, like a madness, like a fiction).

Disastrous evening with Vincent. He makes me smoke some weed that puts me in a mad state of desire, and then tells me off. He says that we don't believe in the same things, since he doesn't believe in anything, neither love nor literature, in God even less, barely in the beauty of the sea or the snow. He wants to make me eat my pornographic comics and says he'll eat my book that I just gave him, devour the edges before attacking the inky parts, which are more bitter.

For an hour, Vincent talks to me about a wave—how to take it, how to ride it or be crushed by it, how to be at one with it; I tremble with fear, feeling death coil between us.

1985   Vincent upon returning from Africa: a leper. Holes in his skin, on his fingers, on his chin. Depigmentation of certain zones on his back. He scares me. He asks to sleep with me. For the first time, he caresses me.

Sleepless nights. Fleeting dreams, almost swoons, that return Vincent's prick to me or cause me to suffocate.

Dream of Vincent's skin.

I've been telling myself all this time: if Vincent were to call me, I must absolutely keep myself from seeing him (I'm convinced that I've been infected); he just called and I actually managed, cheerfully, to make the nicest excuses to avoid seeing him. His voice remains such a comfort.

Definitive inability to cruise: instead, draw up contracts for prostitution (propose to Vincent that he be my geisha—my geisho?).

1984   The sexual control of an implacable but defiable and languishing refusal: the child is the master of this game; he presents himself innocently but imperiously, as an expert in my gratification. He chose for me a pair of impenetrable black pants whose only opening exposes a stretch of skin running down the groin; he makes me storm it as if it were a barricade, fighting the resistance of his fingers. Just sniff the hard prick under the fabric. When the mouth—lips and voice—has been subjected to a sufficient number of supplications, the nimble hand strips away the pants like a theatrer prop. Contemplation of the young sex, pink and soft, milky, barely veined, bouncing in his hand. As his eyes tease, his other hand goes to rob the stash in the crocodile valise where my pornographic magazines, dildo, and whip are hiding. Sublime agitation in the refusals of pleasure.

That furious desire (obtuse and glorious, lamentable) for cock, which must be more general, for genitalia, for pussy (I heard Vincent fantasizing about it aloud the other night, when I was sucking him off), isn't it just as abstract and primordial as the desire for the book or the painting?

Pleasure in taking the suspender off his naked shoulder (imagination of the pleasure men take in undressing women).

Barely slept, fully dressed on top of my bed, with the lights on, but in Vincent's arms, happy with each return of his hand to my body, happy that our mouths always seek each other out unconsciously when they should be defeated, and smile at each other. Strangeness and joy of such a resurrection (opium?)

1983   Phantoms (Vincent, then Eugène) who unfairly eclipse
the present ones.

More and more unbearable, not to listen to the voice
that reminds me of love. And so I remember how, in
that hotel in Madrid, I kissed his groin while he pulled
down his sweater to keep me from his cock. How I
came, while watching him jerk off naked, far away from
me, and while crying (but all of this is unspeakable).

In Spanish restaurants: never felt so much hatred
towards me: I'm going out with a child too old to be my
son, too young to be my brother.

I go again with him to all the sites I visited two or
three years ago with T: the Molino, the cable cars
above the port of Barcelona, the mountain with the
amusement park. At the Hotel Colon, I recognize a
bellboy in a striped uniform who had shown some
interest the last time; I can see in his eyes that he
remembers T. when he looks at Vincent. When we
leave the hotel, he stops us, out of breath, holding out

a small leather glove; he says that he found it between our sheets. It's Vincent's glove.

We had a date to meet at the train station, in front of the Talgo, he startled me; he was horribly dressed, wearing only his father's clothes, right down to the hideous printed silk scarf.

The child, again (but he's almost no longer a child: his body has grown, hairs have appeared on his pubis): I stroke his bare feet while he draws me, the concentration of the drawing anesthetizes his feet.

He kept bugging me to give him *Les Chiens*, my pornographic novelette; I tell him it's not a story for children, manage to forget his request for two nights in a row; on the third, he steals the book from me; the day after, he calls to tell me that he read it on his bike on the way home, under the glow of the streetlights.

I remember that voice that I had mourned: in this empty center of a Sunday, it resurrects the love for the one in whose throat it nestles.

Grief of the illusion of this love.

1982   He said, I had decided not to love men any more, but you I really liked.

ABOUT THE AUTHOR

Hervé Guibert was the author of more than twenty-five books, many of which redefined the genres of fiction, criticism, autobiography, and memoir. A photography critic for *Le Monde* from 1977 to 1985, he was also a photographer and filmmaker in his own right, and in 1980 published the photonovel *Suzanne and Louise*, a book that combined photographic studies of his great-aunts with stories about them. In 1984 he was awarded a César for best screenplay in partnership with Patrice Chereau for *L'Homme Blessé*. Shortly before his death, he completed *La Pudeur ou L'impudeur*, a video work that chronicles the last days of his life while living with AIDS. He died in 1991, at the age of 36.